Once there was Queen Elizabeth, perhaps the wisest ruler
England has ever had. She was not just the most powerful woman
in the world—she was the most powerful person in the world.

Once there was Joan of Arc. She carried a sword and led men in battle. She was on what she believed to be a holy mission for France. She was . . . kind of intense.

Once there was Rosie the Riveter. She was a fictional character used by the U.S. government. She worked in a factory during World War II while men were off at war. She was patriotic. She was strong.

And now there is . . .

Hillary

by Jonah Winter

illustrated by Raul Colón

schwartz & wade books · new york

There was once a girl named Hillary Rodham who did well in school, played sports with the boys, and liked to be in charge. She grew up in a suburb of Chicago with two brothers, a mother, and a father who bossed them all around. Hillary sometimes stood up to him. She was scrappy.

Hillary's mother was a traditional wife and mother. She kept the house clean and cooked all the meals while her husband made all the money *and* important family decisions. She was born at a time when women in the United States weren't even allowed to vote. That's how it was.

Still, both parents believed that their daughter should have every opportunity their sons had. They encouraged Hillary to go to college, which she did—to an all-girls' school. And when she graduated, she became the first student ever to give a speech at the ceremony, where she criticized the school's guest speaker and spoke out against war—and wound up in *Life* magazine one week later. There was no doubt about it: Hillary was a force to be reckoned with—

a fact that was clear to all who met her at law school. It was especially clear to a fellow student named Bill Clinton, who fell in love with her.

Hillary was pretty fond of Bill, too. So just like her mother, she became a wife, marrying this man who would go on to great heights.

And just like her mother, Hillary became a mother—she and Bill had one daughter, Chelsea, whom they adored.

At the same time Hillary was taking on marriage and motherhood, many women were taking to the streets, demanding equality. As part of the women's liberation movement, they were asking: *Why shouldn't we make as much money as men? Or be hired for the same jobs as men? Or be in charge, like men?* These questions were much on Hillary's mind.

And so, though her husband was elected governor of Arkansas, a place where most folks expected her to stand quietly in his shadow, Hillary was not about to give up her career as the first female lawyer at her law firm. After all, she was the chief breadwinner for her family— no small accomplishment.

But Hillary wanted more out of life than a good career. What she wanted was to change the world. And so, when her husband was elected president of the United States and she became First Lady, Hillary was not to be like other First Ladies.

She became the *first* First Lady to have her own office in the important West Wing of the White House. She became the *first* First Lady to head up her own government task force (with a staff of over five hundred) devoted to making health care available to *all* Americans—a mission at which many men before her had failed. She learned everything she could about health care and presented those facts to Congress as no other person in history had done. And though she too failed, she showed America just who Hillary Rodham Clinton was.

And Hillary didn't stop there. She went to China and gave a courageous speech about the way women and girls were being treated around the globe. She said that "women's rights are human rights."

She became the *first* First Lady to run for political office and to be elected to the United States Senate, representing New York State, where she served when her husband was no longer president. Out of one hundred senators, she was one of only thirteen women.

But why stop at the Senate? Hillary was the *first* First Lady to run for president!

And if you're going to run for president, you must be
strong, you must be tough, you must be confident, you
must be competitive—even if it means you may be hated
by millions of people. Some of these people sit behind
radio microphones, and others shout on television news
shows. But you must take it, like a boxer takes blows to
the stomach. If you want to be president, you do not give
up without a fight. Hillary didn't—not until the last vote
was counted and she had lost the Democratic primaries
to a man named Barack Obama. But no woman had ever
come as close to being president.

And if you want to change the world, you've got to be able to bounce back from defeat. Hillary bounced back . . . into one of the most important jobs in the world—*secretary of state,* in charge of America's relations with all other nations. It was a job in which she could make a difference, especially for girls and women. Hillary now had the biggest audience she'd ever had. Her words mattered as they never had before.

Hillary got this job because she was the best one for it. Having spent sixteen years in the White House and the Senate, she knew more about the world than most people—and was more respected around the world than most people. Only the third woman ever to be secretary of state, she immediately made her mark.

She was the hardest of workers, getting up earlier and staying up later than anyone, reading countless reports filled with important information, making decisions that might save lives or cost lives,

meeting with foreign leaders from the mightiest countries, such as
Russia, speaking clearly and courageously,

and meeting with foreign leaders from the tiniest countries, too, such as Brunei, and giving them the same attention she gave to all other leaders as the United States' chief ambassador.

In Egypt, where women do not have as many rights as men, she gave a speech that called for equality between men and women. She was challenged by men in the audience: how dare she come to Egypt and tell them what to do? Hillary did not back down.

In Cambodia, where only a tiny percentage of girls are allowed to go to school and women are expected to walk so quietly as not to make a sound, Hillary said, "Millions of women here in Southeast Asia are trapped . . . laboring in fields and factories for very low wages. . . . Women [should] be given the same rights as men and the same dignity so that they can fulfill their own God-given potential."

There are those who say that talk is cheap, that words don't matter, that actions speak louder than words. But words can *be* actions—if said in the right place at the right time by the right person. A Cambodian, Mu Sochua, said that hearing Hillary's words years ago gave her the courage to go into politics and fight for women's rights. "Watching her," Sochua said, "I had the sense that I could do it, that other women could do it."

You've got to be tough to keep up a schedule of nearly constant travel—up in the air, wearing your sunglasses, checking your smartphone, your tray table piled high with reports to be read.

You hardly sleep at all, so exhausted you can barely stand, visiting country after country after country—and you keep on going.

You break your elbow—and keep on going.

You collapse onstage and get a concussion—and after some rest, you keep on going.

After that concussion, Hillary returned to a hero's welcome from her staff. She was presented with a football helmet and a jersey that said "112." That's because she had visited 112 countries, *more than any secretary of state in history*.

What kind of person sets such a record? A person who is unstoppable.

Hillary may not be Queen Elizabeth. But she may soon change the world—into a place where a girl can dream of growing up to be president, a place where men and women are equal.

Author's Note

On October 26, 1947, Hillary was born to Dorothy and Hugh Rodham in Chicago. When she was three years old, her family moved to the upper-middle-class suburb of Park Ridge. Her relationship with politics started in high school, when she joined a Republican club called the Goldwater Girls, campaigning door-to-door for Republican presidential candidate Barry Goldwater, a vocal supporter of foreign military intervention. During this period, she also became involved with the Methodist Church, which would remain an important part of her life. In a church study group for teenagers, her mentor introduced her to the words and deeds of the Reverend Martin Luther King Jr., whose advocacy for the poor and downtrodden would have a huge impact on the values she embraced as an adult— values that would ultimately lead her to a lifelong membership in the Democratic Party.

To this day, Hillary continues to be shaped by these early interests and passions: compassion for those who are less fortunate in our world, along with a tough-minded, sometimes militaristic streak often associated with Republicans such as Hillary's girlhood hero Barry Goldwater. In 2002, as a U.S. Senator, she voted in favor of America's military invasion of Iraq. As secretary of state, she was opposed to bringing American troops home from Iraq and ending that war.

Hillary Clinton's main focus as a public servant has been advocacy for women and children around the world. And her record on this score is lengthy. Just out of law school, she worked for the Children's Defense Fund in Cambridge, Massachusetts. A few years later, in 1977, she cofounded the Arkansas Advocates for Children and Families. As First Lady, she helped create the Justice Department's Office on Violence Against Women in 1994. And in 1997, she threw her full support behind the State Children's Health Insurance Program, which helps provide health care for poor children. More recently, Hillary founded a global project for the advancement of girls and women called No Ceilings, which works to assess the progress girls and women have made since the Fourth World Conference on Women in Beijing in 1995, at which Hillary gave an often-quoted speech.

What drew me to this topic: Many people, including me, are ready and eager to see a woman be president of the United States. With her experience and popularity, Hillary strikes many of us as the one to make that happen. By becoming president, she would demonstrate that a girl can grow up to be the most powerful person in the world. That's the world where I want to live. And this is a story I am thrilled to tell.

For my mother, who has waited long enough
for this moment —J.W.

In memory of Ramona —R.C.

Text copyright © 2016 by Jonah Winter
Jacket art and interior illustrations copyright © 2016 by Raul Colón

All rights reserved. Published in the United States by Schwartz & Wade Books, an imprint of Random House
Children's Books, a division of Penguin Random House LLC, New York. Schwartz & Wade Books and the
colophon are trademarks of Penguin Random House LLC.

Visit us on the Web! randomhousekids.com
Educators and librarians, for a variety of teaching tools, visit us at RHTeachersLibrarians.com

Library of Congress Cataloging-in-Publication Data
Winter, Jonah.
Hillary / Jonah Winter, Raul Colón. — First edition.
pages cm
Audience: Ages 4 to 8.
ISBN 978-0-553-53388-0 (hc) — ISBN 978-0-553-53389-7 (glb) — ISBN 978-0-553-53390-3 (ebook)
1. Clinton, Hillary Rodham—Juvenile literature. 2. Presidents' spouses—United States—Biography—Juvenile
literature. 3. Women cabinet officers—United States—Biography—Juvenile literature. 4. Cabinet officers—
United States—Biography—Juvenile literature. 5. United States. Department of State—Biography—Juvenile
literature. 6. Women legislators—United States—Biography—Juvenile literature. 7. Legislators—United
States—Biography—Juvenile literature. 8. United States. Congress. Senate—Biography—Juvenile literature.
9. Women presidential candidates—United States—Biography—Juvenile literature. 10. Presidential
candidates—United States—Biography—Juvenile literature. I. Colón, Raul. II. Title.
E887.C55W57 2016
352.2'93092—dc23
[B]
2015005373

The text of this book is set in Mrs. Eaves.
The illustrations were rendered in watercolor, colored pencils, and lithograph crayons on watercolor paper.

MANUFACTURED IN MALAYSIA
2 4 6 8 10 9 7 5 3 1
First Edition
Random House Children's Books supports the First Amendment and celebrates the right to read.